JEKYLL AND HYDE

by Robert Louis Stevenson

CEFR level B1

**Adapted by Karen Kovacs
for
Read Stories – Learn English**

Read Stories – Learn English

Jekyll and Hyde: CEFR Level B1 (ELT Graded Reader)
Original text by Robert Louis Stevenson
Adapted text © Karen Kovacs, 2023
Logo © Karen Kovacs, 2023

No part of this book may be reproduced, scanned or distributed in any printed or electronic form without permission. Please do not participate in or encourage piracy of copyrighted materials in violation of the author's rights. Thank you for respecting the hard work of the author.

CONTENTS

What are graded readers?	Page 4
Meet the author	Page 5
People in the story	Page 7
The story	Page 9
More stories	Page 82
Exercises	Page 84
Words from the story	Page 85

WHAT ARE GRADED READERS?

Graded readers are books in easy English. They are written for learners of English and use **vocabulary and grammar at your level**.

Each book also includes some new, more difficult words. There are **definitions** for these words at the back of the book.

WHY READ GRADED READERS?

- Studies show that learners who read in English **improve in all areas much faster** than learners who don't read.

- You **don't need a dictionary** so reading is **relaxing**.

- The stories are all in **modern English**.

- You learn vocabulary and grammar **in context** (this is the best way, according to teachers).

- Reading a book in English improves your **comprehension, fluency** and **confidence**.

- Graded readers are not exercises. They are **real stories** you can enjoy, helping you **learn English naturally**.

Meet
the author

I'm Karen, a writer from England.

I have a Degree in English Literature and a Master's in Linguistics. I've taught English in the UK and abroad.

I speak Hungarian, French and Spanish, so I understand how it feels to learn a new language.

I hope you enjoy this book.

Karen Kovacs

ReadStories-LearnEnglish.com

Other stories at the same level

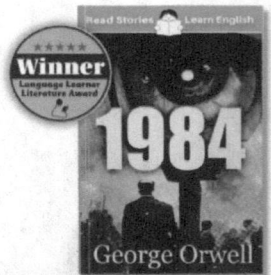

New words

When you see a word in **bold**, go to the back of the book. There you will find a definition of the word.

People in the story

Mr Gabriel Utterson
Mr Richard Enfield
Dr Henry Jekyll
Mr Edward Hyde
Dr Hastie Lanyon
Poole
Sir Danvers Carew
Mr Guest

Chapter 1
The story of the door

Mr Gabriel Utterson was a lawyer. He was tall and thin, and he never smiled. He had a calm, quiet personality and did not often show his emotions. When he talked, he used very few words. He lived a simple life and didn't spend a lot of money on himself. He didn't drink expensive wines and, although he enjoyed the theatre, he never went.

Despite all this, his friends loved him. He was a good man and very kind. If his friends had a problem, they often came to him and Utterson always tried to help them, instead of **judging** them.

Mr Utterson's friends were either family or very old friends. His best friend was Richard Enfield, who was also his cousin. The two men were completely different and people often wondered how they could be friends. Mr Enfield was lively and sociable and was seen at every party in London.

Every Sunday, these two friends went for a **stroll**. During these walks, they usually didn't speak and they often looked bored. However, the friends enjoyed the walks very much and looked forward to them all week.

On one of their Sundays strolls, they walked down a **side street** in a busy part of London. The street was small and quite quiet but there were lots of shops on it. Of course, these were closed on Sundays so the street was almost empty now. The shops were neat and tidy, and they made the street look very pleasant. It was nicer than most of the other streets nearby. The people who lived here were not rich but they lived quite well.

Two doors from one corner, on the left-hand side of the street, there was an entrance to a **court**. And just at that point, there was a **sinister** building. It was two **storeys** high and had no windows. It was in a bad condition and it was obvious that, for a very long time, nobody had taken care of it.

Mr Enfield and the lawyer were on the other side of the side street but, when they passed that building, Enfield pointed and said, "Have you ever noticed that door?"

"Yes, I have," answered Mr Utterson.

"It is connected in my mind," Mr Enfield said, "with a very **odd** story."

"Is it?" Utterson said, some interest in his voice. "And what story is that?"

"Well, this is what happened," Enfield explained. "It

was around three o'clock on a black winter morning and I was coming home from a party. I walked down street after street, and they were all empty because everyone was asleep. All I could see were streetlamps – rows and rows of streetlamps. I didn't feel safe and began to feel nervous, almost wishing to see a policeman. Suddenly, I saw two people moving towards a corner from two different streets. One was a little man, walking quickly. The other was a little girl, about eight or ten, and she was running. When they arrived at the corner, they crashed into each other."

"Oh dear," said Mr Utterson quietly.

"No, wait," replied his friend. "That's not the horrible part. The man trampled over the child's body as she lay screaming on the ground. It was terrible to see. He didn't care at all and just carried on walking. Can you believe it? He didn't seem human."

"What did you do?" asked the lawyer.

"I shouted 'Hey!' and ran after him. I grabbed him by the collar and brought him back to the corner, where there was already a group of people around the screaming child. The man seemed completely calm but he had a cruel **expression** when he looked at me. It made me start **sweating**. The group of people were the girl's own family. They had taken their daughter to see the doctor that night and the doctor himself soon arrived. After looking at her, the doctor announced, 'She's alright. She's not **injured**, only frightened.'"

"Is that the end of the story?" asked Utterson.

"No, it isn't," said Enfield, "because a strange thing happened. We all hated that man. I hated him and the child's family hated him, although that's not surprising. But the doctor *did* surprise me. He was a serious man without strong emotions, it seemed to me. Doctors are used to stressful situations. But when I looked at him, I could see that he was extremely angry with the man. He was so angry that his face was **pale**! I knew what was in the doctor's mind and he knew what was in mine. We couldn't kill him so what could we do instead?"

Mr Utterson listened carefully to his friend, who continued, "We told the man, 'We will tell everyone in London what you did. There will such a **scandal** that your **reputation** will be destroyed forever and you will lose all your friends.' **Meanwhile**, the women in the group were looking at him with anger in the eyes. They even tried to attack him a few times but we prevented them.

And, in the middle, there was the man, with a cold, hard expression on his face, like a **devil**. But I could see that he was, in fact, scared. 'You want to make money out of this accident, do you?' he said. 'Well, I don't have a choice, do I? What can I do? I don't want a scandal so I have to pay you. How much do you want?'"

"How much money did he promise?" Utterson asked.

"A hundred pounds for the child's family," replied Mr Enfield. "He wasn't keen but we all insisted. Next, he had to get the money. And where do you think he took us?"

"To that **dingy** door?" guessed Utterson, looking towards the door opposite them.

"Exactly," said Enfield. "He took out a key, went in and came back to us with some cash and a cheque. On the cheque, there was a name that I won't mention now. But it's a name that is well known."

"What a story!" cried Mr Utterson.

"Yes, it's a terrible story," said Enfield. "That man was cruel but the other man who wrote the cheque is a good man. Why did he write the cheque for him? It's **blackmail**, I suppose. He's an honest man now but perhaps he behaved badly when he was younger. This cruel devil is blackmailing him and the good man doesn't want a scandal."

"Does the man that you hate live in that building?" Utterson asked, looking across the street.

"It would seem likely, wouldn't it? The place is dark and

ugly, like him. But no, he doesn't. He lives in a square somewhere."

"Did you ask him about this building here, with the door?" asked the lawyer.

"No, I don't like to ask too many questions," replied his friend. "But I have looked carefully at it many times. It doesn't even seem to be a house. There's no other door and nobody goes in or out except, very rarely, that man. There are three windows on the first floor that **look onto** the court but there are no windows on the ground floor. The windows are always shut but they're clean. I suppose somebody lives there."

The pair continued their stroll for a while in silence. Then Mr Utterson said, "I know you think it's not good to ask too many questions but I want to ask you the name of that man who trampled over the girl."

"Well," said Mr Enfield, "I don't think it matters if I tell you his name. It's Mr Hyde."

"Hmm," said Utterson. "And what does he look like?"

"He's not easy to describe," started the friend. "There is something wrong with his appearance, something very unpleasant – I hated him as soon as I looked at him but I don't know why. He's very strange-looking but I can't explain the reason why. No, I can't describe him. And it's not because I can't remember him – I remember him very clearly."

Mr Utterson again walked a little distance in silence. He was obviously thinking hard. At last, he asked, "Are you sure he had a key?"

Yes, I'm sure. And he still has it. I saw him use it again a week ago." Enfield **hesitated** and then began, "Utterson …"

"Yes?" replied his friend.

"Why haven't you asked me the name of the other man, the one who wrote the cheque?" asked Enfield.

"Because I already know it," said the lawyer.

Mr Enfield was surprised and a little annoyed with his friend. "Why didn't you tell me that before?" he asked. But he didn't wait for an answer. Instead, he said, "Let's never talk about this again."

"No problem at all," said the lawyer.

"Let's agree and shake hands," said Mr Enfield. And so they did.

Chapter 2
The search for Mr Hyde

That evening, Mr Utterson went home in a serious mood. He sat down to eat his dinner without enjoying it.

Usually, on a Sunday evening after dinner, he sat by the fire and read a book until midnight, when he went to bed. On this night, however, he picked up a candle and went into his home office. There, he opened his **safe** and took a document from the most secret part of it. He sat down to look at the document.

On it were the words 'Doctor Jekyll's **Will**'. Mr Utterson was Dr Jekyll's lawyer. He had agreed to keep the will in his safe for Dr Jekyll, although Utterson had refused to help him write it.

The will said: "When I, Doctor Henry Jekyll, die, give everything that I own to my friend Mr Edward Hyde. If I disappear, or if I am absent for longer than three months, Mr Edward Hyde must **inherit** everything that I own."

"This will **troubles** me, as a lawyer and as someone who prefers sensible things," thought Utterson. "The will troubled me even before I knew who Mr Hyde was. And now, it troubles me even more!"

As he put the will back in the safe, he remembered the story of Mr Hyde, the devil. Mr Utterson said to himself, "Previously, I thought the will was crazy but now, I think it's dangerous."

The next moment, he blew out his candle, put on his coat and walked in the direction of Cavendish Square. That is where his friend, the brilliant Dr Lanyon, lived and it was also where Lanyon saw his patients. "Lanyon knows everyone," Utterson thought. "I'll ask *him* about this."

Dr Lanyon's very serious **butler** knew and welcomed Utterson. Without any delay, he took the guest to the dining room, where Dr Lanyon sat alone with a glass of wine. Lanyon was a lively, cheerful, red-faced man. The two men were old friends – they knew each other from school and university – so when Lanyon saw Utterson, he jumped up from his chair and happily welcomed him with both hands.

After chatting for a few minutes, Mr Utterson introduced the topic that was on his mind. "You're friends with Henry Jekyll, aren't you?"

"We're old friends," replied Dr Lanyon, "but I hardly ever see him these days."

"Oh really?" asked Mr Utterson, surprised. "I thought you were very close friends?"

"We used to be," said the doctor, "but about ten years ago, he became very odd. His mind became ... sick."

"What do you mean?" asked the lawyer.

"He's a scientist, like me," explained Lanyon, "but he started believing in silly, **unscientific** ideas! A scientist should not believe in crazy things like that." He was angry and his face went suddenly purple.

"Is that all?" Utterson thought. "They just have different scientific ideas." To Lanyon, he said, "Have you ever heard the name of his friend, Mr Hyde?"

"Mr Hyde?" repeated Dr Lanyon. "No, never. Perhaps he's a new friend."

That was the only information that Utterson took back to his big, dark bed. He couldn't sleep that night and he got no rest. At six o'clock the next morning, he was still thinking and thinking in his bed. His imagination was a prisoner of Enfield's story.

In the dark room, he saw **images** in his mind. He saw the city's many streetlamps, then a man walking quickly, then a child running from the doctor's. Then these two people crashed into each other and that devil trampled over the child and carried on walking, not caring about her screams.

At other times during the night, Utterson saw different images in his mind. This time, he saw his friend, Jekyll, asleep in his bed, dreaming and smiling at his dreams. Then the door of that room opened and a man appeared at his side. This man **had power over** Jekyll and told him, although it was the middle of the night, "Get up now and do what I tell you!"

These images went through his mind all night. He only slept for a very short time and, while he slept, he dreamt that he saw a man trampling over a screaming girl at every corner of every street.

The man who did this in his dreams had no face. And, for this reason, Utterson began to feel that he really wanted to see the face of the real Mr Hyde. Then maybe Utterson would forget about all this because it would no longer be such a mystery. Maybe he would finally understand why his friend wanted Hyde to get everything after his death. At least his face would be worth seeing – a cold, cruel but interesting face.

From that time, Utterson began to wait outside the door in the side street with the shops ... in the morning before he went to work, at noon when he stopped for lunch and at night, under the foggy city moon. At all times of the day, the lawyer was there.

"Mr *Hyde* is trying to *hide* from me," he thought, "but I will find him."

At last, Utterson saw him. It was ten o'clock on a cold, dry night. The shops were closed, the streets were empty and the lamps left a regular pattern of light and shadow on the ground.

In the silence of the night, Mr Utterson suddenly heard **footsteps**. Somebody was walking towards the door. Utterson moved quickly into the entrance to the court.

The footsteps came nearer and became louder. The lawyer, looking out from the court, could see the man who made these sounds. The man was small and very plainly dressed. Utterson didn't like him although he didn't know why. The man walked to the door and took a key from his pocket.

Mr Utterson stepped out and touched him on the shoulder as he passed. "Are you Mr Hyde?"

Mr Hyde moved back with fear in his eyes. But his fear did not last long. Although he didn't look into the lawyer's face, he answered calmly, "That is my name. What do you want?"

"I see that you're going into that house," replied the other man. "I'm Mr Utterson of Gaunt Street – have you heard my name? I'm an old friend of Dr Jekyll's and I hope I can come in."

"Dr Jekyll is not at home," said Mr Hyde. Then suddenly,

but without looking up, he asked, "How do you know me?"

"Before I answer you," said Utterson, "will you do me a favour?"

"Yes, alright," said Mr Hyde.

"Will you let me see your face?" asked Mr Utterson.

Mr Hyde hesitated for a moment but then he turned around confidently and the pair stood looking at each other for a few seconds. "Now I'll recognise you if I see you again," said Utterson. "It may be useful one day."

"Yes," replied Mr Hyde. "It's good that we met. And you should have my address." He told Utterson his address, which was in Soho, London.

"Thanks," said Utterson.

"And now tell me," continued Hyde, "how did you know me?"

"A friend described you to me," answered the lawyer.

"Who?" asked the man.

"We have common friends."

"Common friends? Who are they?" asked Mr Hyde, a little **gruffly**.

"Dr Jekyll, for example," answered Utterson.

"Dr Jekyll didn't tell you about me!" cried Hyde. "You shouldn't tell lies!" And the next second, he unlocked the door and disappeared into the house.

Utterson stayed in the street for a while after Mr Hyde left him, feeling anxious. Then he began to walk up the street, pausing after every step or so and putting his hand to his face. What worried him was this: he thought, "Why do I hate that man so much? He has a cruel smile, that's true. He seems nervous and confident at the same time. And his voice has an unpleasant, gruff sound. But all this doesn't give me a reason to hate him."

Then Utterson thought, "There is something more. But what?" Utterson thought about it for a moment, then realised, "It's that the man seems hardly human! Oh, my poor old Henry Jekyll! Your new friend has the face of a devil."

Round the corner of the side street, there was a square of smart, old houses. Utterson stopped outside one of these houses, the second from the corner. It was a large, expensive, comfortable house all in **darkness** now except for one small light coming from inside.

Mr Utterson knocked. A well-dressed elderly butler opened the door.

"Is Dr Jekyll at home, Poole?" asked the lawyer.

"I will check, Mr Utterson," said Poole and, as he spoke, he led the man into a large, warm hall. "Wait here by the fire, please, sir."

Utterson had always really liked this pleasant room but tonight, standing there, he **shuddered**. Hyde's face sat heavily on his mind. He felt sick and miserable, which was unusual for him. And in this bad mood, he seemed to see something sinister in the firelight and in the shadows on the ceiling.

He was pleased when the butler Poole returned to announce that Dr Jekyll was not at home.

There was a yard at the back of Jekyll's house and Utterson knew there was an old doctor's laboratory across this yard. And *this* was the sinister, dingy building that Hyde had entered. The yard connected the laboratory and the house. "I saw Mr Hyde enter by the old laboratory, Poole," Utterson said. "Should he do that when Dr Jekyll is out?"

"It's alright, Mr Utterson, sir," replied the **servant**. "Mr Hyde has a key."

"Your **master** really trusts that man, doesn't he?" asked the other man.

"Yes, sir, he does," said Poole. "And Dr Jekyll always tells us servants, 'Always do what Mr Hyde tells you to do.'"

"I don't think I've ever met Mr Hyde," said Utterson.

"Oh no, sir!" answered Poole. "He never has dinner here.

We rarely see him on this side of the house. He mostly enters and leaves by the laboratory."

"Well, good night, Poole."

"Good night, Mr Utterson."

And the lawyer set off home with a very heavy heart. "Poor Henry Jekyll," he thought. "He's **in trouble**, I'm sure. He was **wild** when he was young. I suppose he did … some bad **deed** … and he wants to keep it a secret. I think Hyde knows about what Jekyll did and is trying to blackmail him. He says there will be a scandal if Jekyll doesn't pay Hyde to stay quiet."

Of course, Mr Utterson didn't know all this for sure but he couldn't see any other explanation for Dr Jekyll's will or the recent events.

The lawyer was scared by the thought and considered his own past, searching every corner of his memory. Had he done anything that he might be punished for? On the whole, he had behaved well when he was younger, more than most men probably. But thinking about the few bad things he *had* done made him feel nervous and he was grateful for the many other bad deeds he had avoided.

Suddenly, Utterson had a happier thought, which gave him hope. "Maybe this Mr Hyde did some bad deeds too," he wondered. "Maybe he has his own dark secrets that would make Jekyll's secrets look like sunshine. Things cannot continue like this. Perhaps I can help Jekyll escape this man. He's very dangerous."

Another thought came to him. "Hyde must never find out about the will because it might make the devil **impatient** to inherit! I have to help Jekyll. But will he let me help him?"

Chapter 3
Dr Jekyll is at peace

It was lucky that, a fortnight later, the doctor gave one of his pleasant dinners to about five or six old friends, all intelligent men and all fans of good wine.

Mr Utterson made sure that he stayed after the others had left. This was nothing new – it had happened many times before. Utterson's friends liked him a lot. They liked to talk to the serious lawyer after the more lively, fun guests had gone. They liked to sit for a while with this quiet man who never judged them. And Dr Jekyll was definitely one of the people who felt this way about Mr Utterson. Jekyll, a large, stylish man, about fifty years old, sat on the opposite side of the **fireplace** from his friend. And you could see from the warm expression on his face as he looked at Utterson that he really liked him.

"I need to speak to you about something, Jekyll," began this friend. "You know your will?"

If you were watching carefully, you might be able to see that the question made Dr Jekyll nervous. But the doctor didn't show it. He just smiled and said, "My poor Utterson!

You're so troubled by my will! You need to relax. You're so stressed sometimes, like our friend Dr Lanyon. He gets very stressed about my 'unscientific ideas' – that's what he calls them."

"Lanyon's a good man," Utterson defended him.

"Oh, I know," agreed Jekyll. "He's an excellent man and I should see him more often. But his ideas are too old-fashioned. He doesn't understand me at all and I'm disappointed in him."

"You know I never liked it," Utterson said seriously, returning to their earlier topic.

"My will? Yes, I know that," said the doctor, **slightly** impatiently. He had stopped smiling now.

"Well, I'm telling you again," continued the lawyer. "I've been finding out things about young Hyde."

Dr Jekyll's handsome face went pale, even his lips, and a darkness came into his eyes. "I don't want to hear any more about this," he said. "I thought we had agreed to avoid this topic."

"What I heard was shocking," said Utterson.

"It won't change anything. You don't understand the situation I am in," replied the doctor. "It's an awful situation, Utterson – my friendship with Hyde is a very strange one. But talking about it won't help."

"Jekyll," said Utterson, "you know me. You can trust me. Tell me your secret and I'm sure I can help you."

"My good Utterson," said the doctor, "you're very kind and I cannot find the words to thank you. I trust you completely. I trust you more than anyone else, even more than myself! But the situation isn't what you think. It isn't as bad as that so let your good heart rest. I will tell you one thing: the moment I choose, I can make Mr Hyde leave. I promise you that. And just one more thing ..."

"Yes?" said Utterson.

"This is a private issue," continued Dr Jekyll, "so can I ask you not to talk about it again?"

Utterson thought for a while, **gazing** into the fire.

"Of course. Don't worry," he said at last, standing up to leave.

"Well, as you introduced this topic and for the last time, I hope," continued the doctor, "there is one thing I would like you to understand. I care about Hyde very much. I know you've seen him and he was probably very rude to you. But I do care about that young man a lot. And if I go away, please promise me that you will make sure that my will is followed. Hyde must inherit everything."

"I will never like him," said the lawyer.

"I'm not asking for that," said Dr Jekyll, putting his hand on the other man's arm. "I'm only asking you to help him when I'm no longer here."

Utterson **sighed**. "Alright," he said, "I promise."

Chapter 4
The murder of Sir Danvers Carew

Nearly a year later, in October, there was a crime that shocked the whole of London. It shocked them because it was extremely **violent** but also because the **victim** was well respected and worked for the government.

Only a few details were known. A female servant, who lived alone in a house not far from the river, had gone upstairs to bed at around eleven o'clock. Although thick fog always covered the city later in the night, the early part of the night was clear. The servant's window looked onto a **lane** and the moonlight shone brightly down onto it.

She sat down on a box by her window and gazed out onto the lane, feeling very relaxed and smiling happily to herself.

Soon she noticed a handsome elderly man with white hair, who was walking in her direction along the lane. And there was another, very short man who was walking towards the first one. The servant didn't pay much attention to him at first.

The two men met just under the servant's window. The older man said 'Hello' politely to the other man and they both stopped. The servant couldn't hear what they were saying but it didn't seem very important. The older man was pointing so it appeared that he was asking for directions. The moon shone on his face as he spoke and the servant reported that he looked like such a kind old man and also quite rich.

Then her eyes moved to the other man and she was surprised to see that it was Mr Hyde. She recognised him because he had visited her master once and she had disliked him straight away.

Mr Hyde had a heavy **cane** in his hand. He didn't respond to the older man but just looked very impatient. Then, suddenly, he became extremely angry and lifted the cane into the air.

The old man took a step back, looking surprised and slightly upset. Then Mr Hyde went completely crazy (said the female servant) and violently hit the man with his cane. The older man fell to the ground, injured. The next moment, Hyde trampled over him and hit him again with the cane. His body jumped about in the road as he was hit and the servant could actually hear his bones break.

The servant was extremely shocked. She called for the police but it was too late: the murderer had disappeared. His victim lay in the middle of the lane, his body badly damaged.

The cane, although it was made from a very hard wood, had broken in two. One half was in the road and the other was gone – probably, the murderer had carried it away with him.

Inside the victim's coat pocket, the police found a wallet and a gold watch. Why hadn't the murderer stolen them? They found no cards or papers except an envelope with the name and address of Mr Utterson on it.

The letter was brought to the lawyer the next morning, before he was out of bed. The police explained what had happened and Utterson said seriously, "Please wait while I dress and then show me the body. I won't say anything until I have seen it."

He ate his breakfast in a hurry and drove to the police station, where they had taken the body.

As soon as he saw the body, Utterson **nodded**. "Yes, I recognise him. This is Sir Danvers Carew."

"Oh my God, sir," cried the police officer. "Is it possible?" He continued, "This will be a huge scandal. Perhaps you can help us find the murderer." And he briefly told Utterson what the servant had seen and showed him the broken cane.

Utterson had already **suspected** that the murderer was

Hyde but when the police officer showed him the stick, he knew for sure. Although it was broken and damaged, he recognised it because he had given it to Henry Jekyll many years before as a present.

"Is this Mr Hyde a short person?" asked the lawyer.

"Very short, sir, and the servant said that he looks like a devil," answered the officer.

Mr Utterson thought for a moment, his head down. Then, raising his head, he said, "Come with me in my taxi. I think I can take you to his house."

It was now about nine in the morning and very foggy. Brown fog covered the whole city as the taxi moved slowly from street to street. In certain parts of the city, the wind blew the fog so it became less thick there and the men could see some daylight. Although it was daytime, most of the lamps were still turned on to help against this strange, sinister darkness.

The fog and the lamps made the city look like something from a nightmare and Utterson's thoughts were also very dark. He looked at the police officer and saw that he felt the same.

As the taxi stopped outside the house in Soho, the fog became less thick and they saw a dirty street, cheap shops and restaurants, and lots of poor children sitting in front of the doors. Many women, of different nationalities, were leaving their homes to have a morning drink in a bar.

The next moment, the fog became thicker again, and very brown, and Utterson could no longer see the awful street. This was the home of Henry Jekyll's friend, the man who was one day going to inherit a huge amount of money.

A female servant with a white face and silver hair opened the door. She had an **evil** face but she was polite. "Yes," she said, "this is Mr Hyde's home but he isn't here. He came home very late last night but now he's gone away again."

"Does he often come and go in the middle of the night like that?" asked the police officer.

"Yes, sir," the woman answered, "there's nothing unusual about it. And he's often absent. Until yesterday, I hadn't seen him for two months."

"I see," said the lawyer. "We would like to see his rooms."

"That's impossible!" cried the woman, shocked.

"Do you know who this is?" Utterson replied, pointing to the police officer. "This is Detective Newcomen from Scotland Yard."

The woman looked suddenly delighted. "Ah!" she said. "Is Mr Hyde in trouble? What has he done?"

Mr Utterson and the detective looked at each other. "Mr

Hyde isn't a very popular person, it seems," Detective Newcomen said. "And now, madam, please let us in so that we can look around."

The house was empty except for the old woman. The men could see that Hyde only used a couple of rooms but these had expensive furniture. There was a cupboard full of wine, plates made of silver and a nice painting on the wall. "That was probably a gift from Henry Jekyll," thought Utterson. "He likes buying beautiful paintings."

Despite this, the rooms were untidy. It looked like Hyde had left in a big hurry. Drawers were pulled out, there were clothes all over the floor and Utterson saw that some papers had been burned.

The detective looked in the fireplace and found a green cheque book – only half of it had been burned in the fire. The other half of the cane was found behind a door. Holding the stick in his hand, the detective said, "I suspected Mr Hyde was the murderer but this proves it."

The pair then went to the bank and were told that Mr Hyde had several thousand pounds in his bank account.

The detective was very pleased. "We'll be able to catch him easily," he announced confidently. "It's strange that he left the walking stick and burned his cheque book. Money is everything to him! But all we have to do now is wait for him at the bank. And we will put up posters around London with his name and face on. It won't be long before we find him."

But making a poster was impossible to achieve. Very few people knew Mr Hyde. Even the master of the female servant had only seen him twice. Hyde's family could not be found. There were no photographs of him and people's descriptions of him were all very different. They only agreed on one thing: the man seemed sinister but they couldn't explain why.

Chapter 5
The letter

It was late in the afternoon when Mr Utterson arrived at Dr Jekyll's door. The butler Poole let him in the house and led him through the kitchen and across the yard, which had once been a garden. They then came to the building that was known as the laboratory.

The doctor had bought the house from a doctor who used to cut up dead bodies in that building. But Jekyll was more interested in chemistry than biology so he used the building at the back of the garden for different purposes.

It was the first time that the lawyer had visited his friend in the laboratory. He gazed curiously around the room as he passed through with Poole. It was dingy and there were no windows on this storey. It was empty and silent so it was strange to imagine the room full of interested students, watching as the doctor cut up the bodies of dead people.

At the other end of the room, there were some stairs, which went up to a red door. Utterson followed Poole up the stairs and through the door. They entered a room, which was Dr Jekyll's private study. There was a big table and a tall mirror, and this storey had three windows looking onto the court.

There was a fire, and a lamp sat on the shelf above the fireplace. This was for extra light because, even inside, the fog lay thickly. There, close to the warm fire, Dr Jekyll sat, looking very ill. He didn't get up to greet his visitor but he held out a cold hand and said, without smiling, "Welcome, Utterson." His voice sounded different.

After Poole had left them, Mr Utterson said, "Have you heard the news?"

The doctor shuddered. "The newspaper boys were shouting about it in the square earlier," he said. "I heard them from my dining room."

"I was Carew's lawyer," said Utterson, "but I'm yours, too. Tell me, are you hiding that evil man?"

"Utterson," Jekyll cried, "I promise I will never see Hyde again! My friendship with him is finished forever. And anyway, he doesn't want my help. You don't know him like I do. Believe me, he will never do any more evil deeds and we will never see him again."

The lawyer listened carefully. He was worried. He didn't like how oddly excited his friend was. "You seem very certain of that. I hope you're right and he won't make any more trouble. If he is found, the police will come and talk to you, I'm sure."

"I'm very certain about him," replied Jekyll. "I'm completely certain although I can't explain why. But I need your advice on something. I've received a letter – should I show it to the police? I don't know what to do. Can I give it to you, Utterson? I'm sure you'll do the right thing. I trust you fully."

"Are you worried that the letter will help the police find Mr Hyde?" asked the lawyer.

"No," said the other man. "I don't care what happens to Hyde. I told you, our friendship is over. I was thinking about my own reputation. This crime has created a scandal and changed people's opinions of me."

Utterson thought for a while. He was surprised that his friend was so selfish but he was also **relieved**. It showed that Hyde didn't have the same power over Jekyll anymore. "Well," he said at last, "let me see the letter."

The letter was written in odd, **upright** handwriting. It was signed, "Edward Hyde". "Dear Jekyll," the letter said, "You've been so kind to me but I haven't been a good friend to you. Don't worry, I am safe and the police won't catch me."

The lawyer liked the letter. It showed that Hyde was perhaps not as evil as Utterson had suspected. "Do you have the envelope?" he asked.

"It was silly of me but I burned it," replied Jekyll. "But it wasn't delivered by the postman. Somebody brought it to the house."

"Shall I keep it and think about what to do with it?" asked Utterson.

"Yes. I want *you* to decide what to do," was the reply. "I'm not confident in myself anymore."

"Alright," said the lawyer. Then he said, "One more question …"

"Yes?" answered Jekyll.

"In your will, it says 'If I disappear, Mr Edward Hyde must inherit everything that I own.' Did Hyde tell you to write that?"

The doctor looked very nervous. He kept his mouth shut and nodded.

"I knew it," said Utterson. "He wanted to murder you and inherit all your money. You're lucky that you escaped him."

"Even more importantly," the doctor cried, "I've **learnt my lesson**. Oh God, Utterson, I've really learnt my lesson!" And he covered his face for a moment with his hands.

On his way out, the lawyer stopped and talked to Poole. "By the way," he said, "there was a letter brought to the house today. Who brought it? Do you know?"

"There was no letter, sir," answered Poole.

The butler's reply made Utterson feel worried again. Poole hadn't seen the letter so it was brought to the laboratory door. Did Hyde deliver it himself? Possibly it had been written in Jekyll's study, above the laboratory. And if that were true, Utterson would have to be careful.

As he walked home, the newspaper boys were shouting, "Shocking murder of a well-known man!" Utterson thought, "Already one good man has died. I don't want the reputation of another to be destroyed by scandal. What should I do?" Utterson was always very independent but he began to think, "I need some advice."

A little later, he was sitting on one side of his fireplace and, on the other side, sat his **clerk**, Mr Guest. Between them, there was a bottle of old wine. The fog still lay on the city and, through these 'fallen clouds', the life of the city was moving, making a sound like the wind. But the room was bright with firelight, and the wine, which had been created on a sunny hillside, helped to make it even brighter.

Utterson often told Guest his secrets. He told more of his secrets to Guest than to anyone else, perhaps even more than he should! Guest had often been to Dr Jekyll's house on business. He knew Poole, the butler, and he probably knew about Hyde. So Guest knew enough to be able to give

Utterson useful advice about the letter.

"It's so sad about Sir Danvers," Utterson said.

"Yes, sir, it is," said his clerk. "Everyone has very strong feelings about it because Sir Danvers was well respected. The murderer, of course, was crazy."

"I would like to hear your views on that," replied his boss. "I have a document here in his handwriting. I have no idea what to do with it. But here it is – a murderer's signature."

Guest's eyes became suddenly bright – he was very interested in handwriting and he began to read the letter. "No, sir," he said, "the man is not crazy. But the handwriting is odd."

"And the writer is odd too, it seems," added the lawyer.

Just then, a servant came in with a note.

"Is that from Dr Jekyll, sir?" asked the clerk, after the servant had left. "I think I recognise the writing. Is it private, Mr Utterson?"

"It's only an invitation to dinner. Why? Do you want to see it?" said the lawyer.

"Yes, please, sir," said the clerk and, putting the two pieces of paper next to each other, he compared them carefully.

"Thank you, sir," he said at last, giving both letters back.

Utterson paused and then asked, "Why did you compare them, Guest?"

"Well, sir," replied the clerk, "the handwriting in both letters is very similar. In many ways, it's exactly the same, except one is upright and the other **leans** to the right.

"That's strange," said Utterson.

"Yes, it is," agreed Guest.

"Please don't talk about this note or the letter to anyone," requested the lawyer.

"I won't, sir," said the clerk.

As soon as Utterson was alone that night, he put the note in his safe and it stayed there. "Why is Jekyll changing his handwriting and writing letters for Hyde?" he thought, very troubled. "Why is he protecting a murderer?" And his blood went cold.

Chapter 6
Doctor Lanyon

Time passed and the police couldn't find Hyde. They promised thousands of pounds in reward money because the death of the well-respected Sir Danvers Carew was felt strongly by everyone. But Mr Hyde had disappeared, almost like he had never existed.

Much of his past was discovered and all of it was bad. There were stories that showed how cruel he was. And there were stories of how violent he was. But nobody knew where he was now. From the time he left his house in Soho on the morning of the murder, he had disappeared.

Slowly, Mr Utterson started to recover from the experience and he worried less. The death of Sir Danvers had been terrible but the result was that Hyde had gone, and that was good. Without that evil man, a new life began for Dr Jekyll. He spent less time alone and more time with his friends. He once again gave, and went to, dinner parties. He was busy and active, and he did good deeds for others. His face seemed more open and brighter. For more than two months, the doctor was at peace.

On 8 January, Utterson had had dinner at the doctor's with a small group of people, including Dr Lanyon. Jekyll had looked from Lanyon to Utterson, smiling, as he used to do when the three men were close friends.

However, on the 12th and again on the 14th, the lawyer wasn't allowed in the house. "Dr Jekyll is staying at home today," Poole said, "and doesn't want to see anyone."

On the 15th, Utterson tried again and Poole again refused to let him in. This was difficult for Utterson because, for the last two months, he had got used to seeing his friend almost daily. On the fifth night, he invited Mr Guest to have dinner with him and, on the sixth night, he went to Dr Lanyon's.

Utterson entered that man's house happily but, when he saw him, he was shocked at the change in the doctor's appearance. It was clear that he was soon going to die. His cheeks, which always used to be pink, were now pale. He was extremely thin. He looked balder and older.

But it was not the changes in Lanyon's body that shocked Utterson the most – it was the expression in his eyes and the difference in his behaviour. He looked … terrified. "I suspect he's afraid of death," thought Utterson to himself, "although that would be surprising as he's a doctor. I suppose, because he's a doctor, he knows that his life is nearly over and this knowledge is frightening to him."

However, when Utterson spoke to Lanyon about his bad appearance, the doctor said in a serious but calm voice, "Yes, I won't live much longer."

Utterson looked sadly at his friend, as he continued, "I have had a shock and I'll never recover. I only have a few weeks left. My life has been pleasant – I've enjoyed it. Well, I used to enjoy it. I sometimes think that if we knew everything, we would be happier to die."

"Jekyll is ill, too," mentioned Utterson. "Have you seen him?"

At that moment, Dr Lanyon's face changed and he held up a **trembling** hand. "I don't want to hear any more about Dr Jekyll and I never want to see him again either," he said in a loud but scared voice. "My friendship with that person is over. He is dead to me so please don't talk to me about him ever again."

"I'm sorry to hear that," Utterson replied. Then after a long pause, he added, "Can't I do anything? We are three very old friends, Lanyon. It's not easy to make new friends at our age."

"Nothing can be done," said Lanyon. "Ask Jekyll."

"He doesn't want to see me," said the lawyer.

"That doesn't surprise me," was the reply. "One day, Utterson, after I'm dead, you may perhaps find out everything about this but I can't tell you. And now, can you sit and talk to me about other things ... please? I'd love you to stay, but if you can't avoid that terrible topic, then go! I can't stand it."

Utterson didn't like to judge his friends or ask too many questions, so he stayed and talked to Lanyon about other things.

As soon as he got home, Utterson sat down and wrote to Jekyll. He complained that he had not been let into the house and he asked why his friendship with Lanyon was over.

The next day brought him a long answer, often very sad, sometimes very **mysterious**. There was no solution to the argument with Dr Lanyon. "I don't blame our old friend," Dr Jekyll wrote, "but I agree with him: we must never meet again. In the future, I want to have a quiet life and stay completely alone. You mustn't be surprised and you mustn't worry about our friendship, if my door is shut to you. You must allow me to live my own, lonely life."

The letter continued, "I am being punished for a mistake I made, and I am in danger. But I can't tell you why. I'm really **suffering**. I didn't think it was possible to suffer this much. There is only one thing you can do for me: do what I ask and don't try to contact me or visit me."

Utterson was amazed. Mr Hyde had left, and the doctor

had become sociable again. A week ago, his future seemed bright. And now, in a moment, friendship and happiness seemed to be destroyed. Such a big and unexplained change was often the result of madness. But, remembering Lanyon's behaviour and words, Utterson knew that there must be another reason.

A week later, Dr Lanyon became very ill and, less than a fortnight later, he was dead. The night after his friend was buried, Utterson, feeling very sad, locked the door to his home office. Sitting by the light of a small candle, he took out an envelope. On it were the words, in Lanyon's handwriting, "Private: for G J Utterson ONLY".

Reading those words, the lawyer was scared to open the envelope. "I've buried one friend today," he thought. "What if this letter will tell me of the death of another one?"

But he decided to be brave and he opened the letter. Inside, there was another envelope. On this one were the words, once more in Lanyon's handwriting, "Do not open until the death or disappearance of Dr Henry Jekyll."

Utterson could not believe his eyes. Yes, it said "disappearance". Like in the crazy will (which Utterson had long ago given back to Jekyll), here again was the idea of a disappearance. But in the will, the idea had come from the sinister Hyde. His reasons for wanting that in the will were obvious. Now the idea was written in Dr Lanyon's handwriting – why had *he* written that?

Utterson felt very curious to know what was inside this envelope. But Lanyon's words told him to wait and Utterson was an honest man so he did exactly that. The envelope slept in his private safe.

Utterson still felt curious – that feeling didn't die in him. But, from that day, he no longer wanted to visit Jekyll. He thought of him kindly but he felt frightened. He still went to his house but, now, he was perhaps relieved that Poole didn't let him in. In his heart, he preferred to stay at the front door, talking to Poole, surrounded by the air and sounds of the city. He didn't want to enter that unhappy house that was like a prison and sit with his lonely friend.

Poole had no good news for Utterson. He said that the doctor spent his days in his study above the laboratory and, sometimes, he even slept there. He was depressed and hardly talked. He didn't read. It seemed that he was very stressed about something.

Poole always said the same thing. Before long, Utterson started going to the house less frequently.

Chapter 7
The meeting at the window

On Sunday, Mr Utterson and Mr Enfield met for their weekly stroll. And once again, they walked through the same side street. When they arrived in front of the door, they both stopped to gaze at it.

"Well," said Enfield, "that story's finished at least. We will never see Mr Hyde again."

"I hope not," said Utterson. "Did I ever tell you that I saw him once and shared your feeling of **terror** towards him?"

"It was impossible to see him and *not* feel terror," replied Enfield. "And by the way, you probably thought I was stupid because I didn't realise that this was the back entrance to Dr Jekyll's house."

"So you found out, did you?" said Utterson. "Yes, I knew already. Let's go into the court and have a look at the windows. The truth is that I'm worried about poor Jekyll. And even outside, I feel it may help him to have a friend near him."

The court was cold and slightly wet. Here, it seemed almost like night-time already although, in the street, there was still a bright sunset. There were three windows on the first floor of the building. The middle one was half-open and, sitting by it was Dr Jekyll. He looked extremely sad, like a prisoner.

"Jekyll!" Utterson cried, looking up at the window. "Are you better?"

"I'm miserable, Utterson," replied the doctor in a sad, tired voice, "very miserable. It won't last long, thank God."

"You stay indoors too much," suggested the lawyer. "You should be outside, doing some healthy exercise like Mr Enfield and me."

Utterson introduced the two men. "This is my cousin, Mr Enfield. Enfield, this is my friend, Dr Jekyll."

Then Utterson went on, "Come now, Jekyll. Get your hat and come for a walk with us."

"That's very kind of you," sighed the other man. "I would like to very much. But no, no, no, it is absolutely impossible. I can't. But Utterson, I'm very glad to see you. This is such a pleasure. I would invite you and Mr Enfield inside but my study is too messy."

"Alright, Jekyll," said the lawyer kindly, "the best thing we can do is to stay down here and speak to you from the court."

"That's just what I was about to suggest," replied the

doctor with a smile. But he had hardly said the words before the smile left his face. And it was replaced by an expression of terror. Seeing it froze the blood of the two men below. They only saw it for a moment because the window was very quickly, and violently, closed. But that moment had been long enough, and they turned and left the court without a word.

In silence, too, they crossed the street and they didn't speak until they reached the next street, which was busier than the other one. Mr Utterson looked at his friend. They were both pale and there was terror in their eyes.

"Oh my God, oh my God," said Mr Utterson.

But Mr Enfield only nodded his head very seriously and carried on walking in silence.

Chapter 8
The last night

Mr Utterson was sitting by the fire one evening after dinner, when Poole came to the house. Utterson was surprised to see him.

"Poole, why have you come here?" he cried. Then, taking a second look at him, Utterson noticed that Poole looked troubled. Utterson asked him, "What's the matter? Is the doctor ill?"

"Mr Utterson," said the butler, mysteriously, "there is something wrong."

"Take a seat, and here's a glass of wine for you," said the lawyer. "Now, don't hurry and tell me what has happened."

"You know that the doctor stays in his study above the laboratory, sir," replied Poole, "like a prisoner. Well, he's in there again and he's not coming out. Sir, it makes me feel very worried. Mr Utterson, I'm afraid."

"Poole, tell me clearly," said the lawyer. "What are you afraid of?"

"I've been afraid for about a week," replied Poole, not answering the question, "and I can't stand it anymore."

Utterson looked carefully at the man and saw that it was true. His appearance had changed – he seemed anxious and scared. And he didn't look at the lawyer – he was looking at a corner of the floor and he hadn't drunk any of his wine. "I can't stand it anymore," he repeated.

"I'm sure you have a good reason for feeling this way, Poole," said Utterson. "I see that there is something really wrong. Try to tell me what it is."

"I think there has been some **criminal** behaviour," said Poole.

"Criminal behaviour!" cried the lawyer. He felt frightened and this made him angry and impatient. "What criminal behaviour? What does that mean?"

"I can't explain it, sir," was the answer, "but will you come with me to the house and see?"

Mr Utterson didn't reply but, instead, he stood up and got his hat and coat. He noticed that the butler looked very relieved when he did that, and he also noticed that he still hadn't tasted his wine. Poole put down the glass and followed the lawyer.

It was a wild, cold night in March, with a pale moon. The wind was blowing so strongly that it made it difficult to talk. Perhaps because of the wind, there was nobody in the streets. "I've never seen this part of London so empty," thought Utterson. "I wish there were some people." He felt anxious. He felt that something bad was going to happen.

When they got to the square with Dr Jekyll's house, it was full of wind and dust. The thin trees were hitting against the houses.

Poole had walked in front of Utterson during the journey but now he stopped in the middle of the pavement. He took off his hat and cleaned his face with his handkerchief. He was sweating but it wasn't from the exercise – it was because he was afraid. His face was white.

"Well, sir," he said, "here we are. I hope there's nothing wrong."

"So do I, Poole," said the lawyer.

The servant knocked on the door and it opened, but only slightly. A voice from inside the house said nervously, "Is that you, Poole?"

"It's alright," said Poole. "Open the door."

The hall, when they entered it, was very bright. The servants had made a huge fire and all the servants, men and women, were standing around it together. When she saw Mr Utterson, a young, female servant started crying and the cook shouted, "Thank God, it's Mr Utterson!" She ran towards him, a relieved expression on her face.

"Why are you all standing here?" asked the lawyer

impatiently. "This is really strange. Why aren't you working? Your master would not be pleased."

"They're all afraid," said Poole.

There was silence. No one said anything, although the female servant cried loudly.

"Be quiet!" Poole said to her. He spoke angrily because he was afraid too. Then he said to a young, male servant, "Get me a candle." To Mr Utterson, he said, "Please follow me, sir," and he led the lawyer towards the yard at the back of the house.

"Mr Utterson," he said, "move slowly and quietly. I want you to hear but I don't want you to be heard. And, sir, if he asks you to go inside ... don't go."

Hearing this mysterious warning, Mr Utterson suddenly felt extremely worried. But he tried to be brave and followed the butler into the laboratory building, through the laboratory and to the bottom of the stairs.

Here, Poole **whispered**, "Stand at the side, sir, and listen." Meanwhile, Poole put down the candle and, although he was obviously terrified, he went up the stairs. He knocked with a trembling hand on the red door.

"Mr Utterson is here to see you, sir," he called. He whispered again to Utterson, telling him to listen.

A voice answered from inside. "Tell him I can't see

anyone," it said impatiently.

"Yes, sir," said Poole and, taking his candle, he led Mr Utterson back across the yard and into the large kitchen.

"Sir," he said, looking into Mr Utterson's eyes, "was that my master's voice?"

"It sounded ... very changed," replied the lawyer, who was very pale.

"Changed? Yes, definitely," said the servant. "I've been his butler from twenty years and I know his voice. That isn't him! He's been murdered! He was murdered eight days ago when we heard him shout. Who's in there instead of him? And why is he staying in there, Mr Utterson?" he asked **desperately**.

"This is a very crazy story, Poole," said Mr Utterson, biting his finger nervously. "If someone has murdered Dr Jekyll, as you say, why is the murderer staying here? That seems very strange."

"I see that you don't believe me, sir," said Poole. "Well, let me tell you something more. The person – or *thing* – that lives in the study has been crying night and day for some sort of medicine. My master sometimes used to write his orders on a piece of paper, put them inside an envelope and then leave them on the stairs. I picked up the envelopes and went to buy what he wanted. This week, we've had a huge number of orders ... and a closed door."

"How about his meals?" asked the lawyer.

"We don't even see anybody when we deliver the meals," answered the butler. "We leave the food outside the door and it's taken into the study secretly when nobody is looking. And, sir, every day, there have been orders and complaints, and I've been sent to all the pharmacies in London. Every time I bring the stuff back, there's another piece of paper telling me to return it because it wasn't pure. And every time, there's another order for a different pharmacy. This medicine is wanted very badly, sir, although I don't know what it's for."

"Do you have any of these bits of paper?" asked Mr Utterson.

Poole felt in his pocket and handed the lawyer a folded note. Utterson, leaning near the candle, looked at it carefully. It was written to a pharmacist. It said, "From Dr Jekyll to Mr Maw. Your last powder was not pure and therefore it was useless for my purposes. Previously, I bought a large quantity from you. Please search everywhere and, if you find any of the same quality, send it to me straight away. The cost does not matter at all. I will pay as much as you want."

So far, it had been more or less a normal letter but, at the end, the writing became messy and it said, "**For God's sake**, find it for me!"

"This is a strange note," said Mr Utterson. Then he added, **suspiciously**, "Why did you open it?"

"I didn't, sir," Poole answered. "The pharmacist was angry and he threw it back at me, like it was dirt."

"And is this definitely the doctor's handwriting?" asked the lawyer.

"Yes, it looks like it," said the servant. Then he continued, "But it doesn't matter about the handwriting. I've seen him!"

"You've seen him?" repeated Utterson, surprised. "And?"

"This is what happened," began Poole. "I walked suddenly into the laboratory from the yard. It seems he had come out of his study to look for a medicine or something. The upstairs door to his room was open and he was downstairs, searching for something. He looked up when I came in, **cried out** and ran upstairs back into his study."

"What did he look like?" asked the other man.

"I only saw him for a minute but I felt terrified. Sir, if that was my master, why did his face look so strange? If that was my master, why did he cry out like a rat and run away from me? I've been his servant for so many years. And then …"

Poole stopped and put his hand over his face.

"This is all very odd," said Mr Utterson, "but I think I understand what's been happening. It's obvious that your master has some kind of illness. He feels awful and he's suffering a lot so it's changed his appearance and even his voice. And that's why he's avoiding his friends and that's why he's desperate to get the medicine. He hopes that, with the correct medicine, he will recover fully. And I hope he's right! This is my explanation. It is sad and worrying, Poole, but it is nothing unusual. So you see, we shouldn't be too anxious."

"Sir," said the butler, becoming pale, "that thing was not my master." He looked around him before continuing, in a terrified whisper, "My master is a tall man but this person was short."

Utterson opened his mouth to disagree with Poole but the servant said, "Oh sir, do you think that I don't know my master after twenty years? No, sir, that thing was not Dr Jekyll. I have no idea what it was but it wasn't Dr Jekyll. And I believe in my heart that there has been a murder."

"Poole," replied the lawyer, "you seem so certain that I feel it is my duty to check. This note seems to prove that the doctor is still alive but I think it is my duty to break down the door and make sure!"

"Yes, Mr Utterson, what a brilliant idea!" cried the butler.

"Who's going to do it?" asked Utterson.

"You and me, sir," was the brave reply. "There's an **axe** in the laboratory," he continued, "and you can take the kitchen **poker**."

The lawyer took the poker, as the butler suggested, and told him, "Poole, do you know, we're about to put ourselves in a lot of danger."

"Yes, probably, sir," replied the servant.

"So let's be honest with each other," said the lawyer. "This creature you saw, did you recognise it? I suspect that you did."

"Well, sir, it left so quickly that I can't be sure," was the answer. "But if you mean, was it Mr Hyde? – well, yes, I think it was! It was the same height and it moved in the same, quick way. And who else could get in through the laboratory door? At the time of Sir Danvers Carew's murder, Mr Hyde still had the key to that door, do you remember, sir? But that's not all. Have you ever met Mr Hyde?"

"Yes," said the lawyer, "I spoke to him once."

"Then you know that there is something odd about him. When you look at him, you feel ... terrible. Your blood goes cold."

"I admit that I felt what you describe," said Mr Utterson.

"Well, sir," continued Poole, "when I saw that ... thing ... in the laboratory, my whole body suddenly felt like ice. I know it doesn't prove anything, Mr Utterson, but I know – I *feel* – that it was Mr Hyde!"

"Yes," said the lawyer, "I feel the same. I knew Dr Jekyll's friendship with that evil man was a bad idea. I believe you. I believe that poor Henry has been killed. And I believe the murderer is still hiding in his victim's study. Come on, let's catch Hyde. Call Bradshaw."

Bradshaw was a male servant. When he came, he was very pale and nervous.

"Be brave, Bradshaw," said the lawyer. "This is a difficult situation for us all. Poole and I are going to break down the red door and enter the room. Meanwhile, if anyone escapes through the back of the laboratory, you must stop them. Take a stick and wait by the laboratory door. We'll wait ten minutes before breaking down the door – that will give you time to get there. Go!"

As Bradshaw left, the lawyer held the poker under his arm and walked into the yard, with Poole following him. It was now dark. The light of the candle trembled as the wind moved it first in one direction, then the other. The men entered the laboratory, sat down and waited. The sounds of

London were all around them but, more nearby, they only heard the sound of footsteps moving around in the private study above them.

"It walks around day and night, sir," whispered Poole. "The footsteps only stop when some new powder comes from the pharmacy. Then there's a short break."

"Do you hear any other noises?" asked Utterson.

"Once I heard it crying!" said the butler.

"Crying?" asked the lawyer, with terror in his heart.

"Yes," replied the butler, "and it sounded so sad that I wanted to cry too."

Ten minutes had passed. They put the candle on a table and, with the axe and the poker in their hands, they went slowly up the stairs.

"Jekyll," cried Utterson in a loud voice, "I must see you." He paused for a moment but there was no reply. "We are suspicious, Jekyll – we think something is wrong and we're going to break the door down!"

"Utterson," said a gruff voice, "for God's sake, don't do it!"

"Ah, that's not Jekyll's voice – it's Hyde's!" cried Utterson. "Come on, Poole, let's break the door down."

Poole hit the door hard with the axe and it made a sound like a wild animal. He hit it four times but the wood didn't break. With the fifth hit, finally the door broke and it fell into the room.

The men stood back a little and looked in. They saw Dr Jekyll's study in the lamplight. There was a large fire burning in the fireplace, some drawers were open and there was a cup of tea on a small table. The room was peaceful.

Right in the middle, there was the body of a man, and it was still moving slightly. The men went close to it, turned it over and saw the face of Edward Hyde. He was dressed in clothes that were much too big for him, clothes that were the doctor's size. He stopped moving. In his hand, there was a glass and there was a strong smell in the air.

"We're too late," Utterson said seriously. "Hyde has killed himself. Now all we have to do is find your master's body."

The two men searched the whole building but they couldn't find Jekyll, dead or alive.

"Maybe he escaped," suggested the lawyer.

They went downstairs and to the back door of the laboratory but it was locked. And they found the key, broken on the floor. "Someone trampled on it a while ago," said Poole.

The two men looked at each other. "I don't understand what has happened, Poole," said the lawyer. "Let's go back to the study."

They went back upstairs in silence and searched the study carefully. On a table, they found various piles of white powder.

"That's the medicine that he kept ordering," Poole said.

They saw a long mirror and gazed into it. "This mirror has seen some strange things, sir," whispered Poole.

"Why did Dr Jekyll have such a large mirror?" asked the lawyer.

"I have no idea, sir," said the butler.

Next, they walked over to a desk. On the desk, there were lots of pieces of paper and also an envelope. The envelope had Mr Utterson's name on it. The lawyer opened it and several pieces of paper fell onto the floor. The first was a will, as odd as the other one, which Jekyll had given back to his friend six months before. But there was one important difference: instead of Mr Edward Hyde, the will contained the name of Gabriel John Utterson.

Utterson looked at Poole and then back at the will. Then he looked at the dead man on the floor.

"I don't understand," he said. "This new will means that *I* will inherit everything, not Hyde. Why didn't Hyde burn it?"

The next piece of paper was a brief note. Utterson read it:

"My dear Utterson, When you find this, I have disappeared. I don't know how it will happen but I'm sure it will happen soon. First, you must read the letter that Lanyon has already given you. Then, if you are brave enough to hear more, read my **confession**. Your friend, Henry Jekyll."

"Where's the confession?" asked Utterson.

Poole reached down and picked a thick envelope up from the floor. "Here it is, sir," he said, as he gave it to Utterson.

The lawyer put it in his pocket. "Don't tell anyone about this letter," he said. "If your master has run away or is dead, we can at least save his reputation. It's ten o'clock now. I have to go home and read these documents in peace. But I'll be back before midnight, when we'll call for the police."

They went out and back into the house, locking the door to the laboratory as they left. Utterson, leaving the servants standing around the fireplace in the hall, walked back to his home office to read the two letters. He hoped they would explain this mystery.

Chapter 9
Doctor Lanyon's story

In the letter that Utterson already had in his safe, he read these words from Dr Lanyon:

———

On 9 January, now four days ago, I received in the evening an envelope from Henry Jekyll. I was surprised because we didn't usually write to each other. I had had dinner with him the night before so what could he have to tell me so soon afterwards? This is what the letter said:

———

10 December

Dear Lanyon,

You are one of my oldest friends and, although we have argued over scientific topics, I think we have always liked each other. Lanyon, tonight, I need to ask you a favour. You must help me!

Please come straight away, with this letter, to my house.

Poole has been told to let you in. Go into my study, making sure you're alone. There is a drawer with the letter E on it. Open the drawer, breaking the lock if you have to. Take out the whole drawer and bring it back with you to your home in Cavendish Square.

This is the first part of the favour. Now the second ... At midnight, when a man knocks at your door, let him. Do it yourself; don't let the servants do it. I hope they will be in bed by that time. I have asked this man to go to your house. Give him the drawer from my study and everything inside it.

I will be forever grateful to you if you do this for me. If you don't do me this favour, I might die or go crazy.

My hand is trembling as I write because I'm so scared that you won't help me. But I hope that you will. Think of me, in a strange place, more anxious than you can imagine.

Your friend, Henry Jekyll.

———

When I finished the letter (wrote Dr Lanyon), I was sure that Jekyll was mad. But I felt I had a duty to help him without judging him. I got a taxi to his house, where the butler was waiting for me. He had also received a letter from Jekyll, telling him what to do. I found the drawer and took it out, with everything inside, returning with it to Cavendish

Square.

Here, I looked carefully at its contents. I found some white powders and a tiny bottle, which had a smelly, blood-red liquid in it. There was also a little book with hundreds of dates written in it. The dates started many years ago but stopped suddenly nearly a year ago. There were some words after the dates, like "double". Once, near the beginning of the book, were written the words, "It didn't work!!!" Clearly, Jekyll had done some experiments on those dates and they had been useless, like most of his experiments. But that was all I knew. How could these objects have an effect on the reputation, or the life, of my crazy friend? And why did I have to see this man in private? I prepared my old gun so that I could protect myself with it when he came, if I needed to.

At twelve o'clock, there was a gentle knock at the door. I opened it and there was a small man. "Have you come from Dr Jekyll?" I asked.

He nodded but hesitated before coming into the house. However, suddenly he saw a policeman walking down the street in the darkness and he hurried inside. This made me feel nervous and, as I followed him into my sitting room, I kept my hand on my gun.

I looked at him carefully now. I had never seen him

before. He filled me with terror although I don't understand why. He looked very odd because his clothes were much too big for him.

My visitor was really anxious. He cried impatiently, "Have you got it? Have you got it?" laying his hand on my arm and shaking me.

His touch made my blood go cold. I said, "Sir, you haven't introduced yourself. Please sit down." I sat down too, trying to act normally, although I was stressed.

He also tried to act normally and said, politely, "I'm sorry, Dr Lanyon, you're right. I'm here to collect, for Dr Jekyll ..." He paused and put his hand to his throat, and I could see, despite his effort to appear calm, he was *extremely* anxious. He continued, "I'm here to collect a drawer."

"There it is, sir," I said.

He jumped up and put his hand to his heart. He looked so desperate that I became worried about him. "Stay calm," I told him.

He looked at me with a terrible smile and looked inside the drawer. When he saw its contents, he was so relieved that he cried out loudly. I watched him with wide eyes.

"Have you got a glass?" he asked.

I got up and gave him one. He thanked me and poured

some of the red liquid from the tiny bottle into the glass, then added one of the powders. The **mixture** was dark red at first, then the colour got brighter and smoke started to come from it. Suddenly, the mixture went dark purple, then green. My visitor watched it carefully, smiled and put the glass on table.

Then he turned to me and said, "Now, tell me: will you leave me alone to drink this mixture or are you too curious? Will you stay and see something amazing?"

I wanted to look calm as I answered but I didn't feel calm at all. "I don't believe that I will see anything amazing but I will stay."

"Lanyon," said my visitor, "you never accept new and different scientific ideas. You only believe in traditional science. But now you will now see that you were wrong. Watch!"

He put the glass to his lips and drank all the liquid in it. He cried out, nearly fell over and held onto the table desperately, his mouth open. As I watched, his face became suddenly black and it seemed to change. The next moment, I jumped up from my seat and stood against the wall, my arms raised up to protect me, my mind terrified.

"Oh my God!" I screamed. There, before my eyes, pale and trembling, was Henry Jekyll!

I don't want to write down what he told me in the next hour. I saw what I saw. I heard what I heard. And now I'm terrified and my mind is troubled. I can't sleep and I know I will die soon. Normal science can't explain what I saw. Do I believe in traditional science anymore? Do I believe what I saw? I don't know.

But I'm sure of one thing: the creature who came to my house in the darkness that night was Hyde. He's the man who the police are searching for, the man who murdered Carew.

Your friend, Hastie Lanyon.

Chapter 10
Henry Jekyll's full confession

Next, Mr Utterson opened and read Dr Jekyll's confession:

My family was rich (wrote Dr Jekyll), so I have always had a lot of money. In addition to this, I always worked hard and people always respected me. So, when I was growing up, it seemed that my future was bright. The worst part of my character was that I was a little too lively – I enjoyed having fun.

People liked me for it but I didn't like that about myself. I preferred to appear serious **in public**. For this reason, I hid my pleasures. I never did anything *very* bad but, despite that, I was ashamed of myself. And, as I got older, I realised that my personality was **split** in two. I had both good and bad parts to my character. However, I had to admit to myself that both sides were a true part of me.

I was already studying science but I soon became interested in studying this idea: that humans are not really one, but two. We have two parts.

I began to think, "The good and the bad both live inside me, but what if those two parts could be split into two different people? Life would be more enjoyable. The bad side of me could do bad deeds without feeling ashamed. And the good side of me could do the good deeds that brought him pleasure, without worrying that his reputation would be damaged by his evil twin.

Of course, this would not be possible with traditional science – it would require new ideas, 'unscientific' ideas, as Lanyon called them. But I wanted to try because it is terrible that the good and the bad exist inside every person and are always 'fighting'.

I waited for a long time before I attempted this experiment. I knew that I might die. I would have to be careful when using the powerful ingredients that I needed. But in the end, I couldn't stop myself from trying because I was so curious to see the results.

I prepared the **potion** but there was one missing ingredient. It was a white powder, which I bought a large quantity of from my local pharmacy. I added the final ingredient to the mixture, watched the smoke rise up and then I drank it all.

I felt horrible pain and I felt very sick – death can't be worse than that, I'm sure. But slowly the pain went away and I noticed that I felt different. I felt younger, lighter, happier. My mind felt **free**. It was full of criminal thoughts. These thoughts were much more evil than my previous bad thoughts had been but I didn't feel ashamed. In fact, I felt delighted. I lifted up my hands, enjoying these new feelings, and suddenly I realised that I was shorter.

There was no mirror at that time in my study. The one that's in my room now was bought later so that I could see myself when I **transformed**. To find a mirror, I had to leave my study. I crossed the yard in the darkness of the early morning. The stars gazed down on me – they had probably never seen anything like me before. I walked through my house, feeling a stranger there, and finally arrived in my bedroom. And there, I saw for the first time the appearance of Edward Hyde.

The evil side of my character was smaller than the good side. After all, I had spent most of my life being good. It was for this reason, I think, that Hyde was shorter and younger than Henry Jekyll. But he looked like a devil and the evil in him showed on his face. However, I didn't hate him when I looked in the mirror because he is also a part of me. I preferred him to the divided face I used to see in the mirror.

I have noticed that, when people meet Hyde, they look

terrified. I think this is because all humans are a mixture of good and evil, so we aren't used to seeing someone who is completely evil.

I didn't spend long in front of the mirror. The second, and very important, part of the experiment was not yet completed. Had I lost the good side of myself?

Hurrying back to my study, I once more prepared and drank the potion, once more felt horrible pain and once more transformed into Henry Jekyll.

I now had two characters and two different appearances. One was completely evil but the other was still the old Henry Jekyll. I was still a mixture of good and bad – I wasn't completely good.

So it was not a good change. Even after I created Hyde, I (Henry Jekyll) still enjoyed being a bit wild sometimes and I still found studying boring. I was also getting older. I didn't like this at all and I kept wanting to transform into Hyde again.

I prepared everything carefully. I bought a house in Soho for Hyde and employed a female servant for him. Then, at home, I told my own servants that a man called Mr Hyde was my new friend. "Let him into the house and always do what he tells you," I said.

Next, I wrote that will, the one you hated so much! Now,

if anything happened to Henry Jekyll, Edward Hyde would be protected.

In public, I could be well respected one moment and, the next moment, I could become Edward Hyde and be completely free. I didn't need to worry because, when Hyde did really bad deeds, I just had to come to my study and drink the potion. Then Hyde wouldn't exist anymore and nobody could catch him!

I trampled over a girl one evening and your friend saw me, Utterson. Then one morning, about two months before the murder of Sir Danvers, I woke up in my bedroom and felt very strange. I didn't understand why. I looked down at my hand and noticed that it wasn't the large, white hand of Jekyll. It was the ugly, hairy hand of Hyde.

I hurried to the mirror and my blood went cold. I had gone to bed as Henry Jekyll but I had woken up as Edward Hyde. How could this be explained?

The ingredients for the potion were all in my study so I had to walk through the house, across the yard and into the laboratory building. I was worried about what the servants would think but then I remembered: I had told them that Hyde was my friend so it wouldn't seem strange to them if they saw me.

Ten minutes later, Dr Jekyll was back. But as I ate my

breakfast, I began to think about the problems with my new, double life. Would Hyde become more and more powerful and would his personality become mine? Was I losing the original, better side of myself?

I now felt that I had to choose between Jekyll and Hyde. I enjoyed the secret pleasures of Hyde but, if I stayed as Hyde forever, I would be hated by everyone and have no friends. So I decided to stay as Jekyll.

For two months, I lived as Jekyll and I tried to be good. But I wanted to feel free again and, at last, I made the potion and drank it.

The devil was even more evil now because he had been hidden for so long. I hit Sir Danvers Carew with the cane and enjoyed it. But suddenly I had a feeling of terror and I ran to the house in Soho. I made the potion and soon I was Jekyll again. And I was so relieved that I cried. I couldn't ever transform into Hyde again because he was in trouble with the police and they would **hang** him. So I had to stay as Jekyll and I was so pleased about that. I locked the back door to the laboratory and broke the key with my foot.

As Jekyll, I tried to be as good as possible because I felt guilty about the horrible murder. You know that, during the final months of last year, I did a lot of good deeds and really enjoyed it. But the dark side of me was still there, inside me.

And it wanted to come out!

One bright, cold January day, I sat in Regent's Park in the sunshine, relaxing and listening to the birds singing. Suddenly, I began shuddering and I felt sick. And then I realised that I felt braver and I didn't care about danger anymore. I looked down – my clothes were very loose and my hands were hairy. I was once more Edward Hyde. A moment before, I had been well respected and loved. And now I was a hated murderer!

The ingredients for the potion were in a drawer in my study. How could I get them? I had locked the laboratory door and, if I entered through the main house, my own servants would call the police and I would be hanged.

I thought of Lanyon. But how could I convince him to help me? Then I realised that I could write in Jekyll's handwriting. I went to a private room in a hotel and asked for a pen and paper. I wrote my two important letters, one to Lanyon and one to Poole, and then I waited alone in that room. I should say "he", not "I".

At last, it was night-time and he walked through the dark streets to Lanyon's house. When I transformed back into Jekyll, I felt sad to see Lanyon's terror. But I felt more strongly that I did not ever want to be Hyde again.

I went home and slept. I woke up feeling weak but a bit

better. I was still afraid of the devil that was inside me but I was back home and close to my potion. I was grateful that I had escaped.

The next morning, I was walking calmly across the yard after breakfast when suddenly I got those strange feelings again. I hurried to my private study before I transformed once more into Hyde. I had to take double the amount of the potion this time in order to transform, but luckily I became Jekyll again.

However, unfortunately, six hours later, as I sat gazing sadly into the fire, I became Hyde and had to take the potion again. From that day, it has been difficult to stay as Jekyll. I transformed into him during the day and, if I slept, I always woke up as Hyde, full of energy and ready to do horrible things. As Jekyll, I was terrified to sleep and I became weak in body and mind. As Jekyll became weaker, Hyde's power over him became stronger.

Hyde loves life so he is scared of being hanged and also scared that I will kill myself, which would kill *him* too. Hyde hates Jekyll. He needs to become Jekyll to escape the police but he dislikes having to do it. He shows me that he hates me by burning my letters and once he even destroyed the painting of my father.

No one has ever suffered as much as me. I am so

miserable.

And there is another problem. I am running out of white powder. I asked Poole to buy me some more but, when I made the mixture and drank it, it didn't work. None of the new powders work. I thought the new ones were not pure but I now believe that, in fact, the original powder was not pure. Some unknown extra ingredient made the potion work.

About a week has passed and I'm now finishing this confession as Jekyll, using the last bit of the old powder. This, therefore, is the last time that Jekyll can think his own thoughts or see his own face in the mirror. I must hurry and finish the letter because, if I transform into Hyde while writing it, he'll burn it.

In half an hour, I will be that horrible man again and I know that I will sit trembling and crying in my chair. I will listen, terrified that someone is coming to catch me. Will Hyde be hanged? Or will he be brave enough to kill himself? I don't know and I don't care. *I* am dying *now* – the other death will not be mine. As I finish this confession and put down my pen, I end the life of this unhappy Henry Jekyll.

THE END

MORE STORIES

A1+ Elementary

A2 Pre-intermediate

B1 Intermediate

B2 Upper intermediate

VISIT MY WEBSITE

You will find:
- **information** about my **other books**
- **free stories**
- **free exercises** for this book
  (vocabulary exercises, comprehension exercises and notes about British culture)

ReadStories-LearnEnglish.com

Words from the story

axe (n)
a tool used for cutting up large pieces of wood

blackmail (v)
make someone give you money or do what you want by threatening to tell people embarrassing information about them (**blackmail**, n)

butler (n)
the most important male servant in a rich person's house

cane (n)
a long thin stick that someone uses when they walk

clerk (n)
someone whose job is to look after the documents in an office

confession (n)
a written statement in which you admit that you have done something wrong

court (n)
a square area that is surrounded by buildings

criminal (adj)
relating to illegal acts

cry out (phr v)
make a loud noise because you're in pain, afraid or shocked

darkness (n)
the lack of light, usually because it is night

deed (n)
something that someone does

desperate (adj)
very worried because you don't know how to deal with an unpleasant situation

devil (n)
an evil spirit

dingy (adj)
dark and dirty

evil (adj)
doing very bad or cruel things

expression (n)
a look on a person's face that shows what their thoughts or feelings are

fireplace (n)
a place in a room where a fire burns

footstep (n)
the sound your feet make when you're walking

for God's sake (phr)
used for showing you are worried

free (adj)
not controlled or limited

gaze (v)
look at something for a long time because it is interesting or because you're thinking of something else

gruff (adj)
(of a voice) unfriendly and low

hang (v)
kill someone by putting a rope around their neck and making them fall (**hanged**, past tense)

have power over (phr)
be able to control or influence someone

hesitate (v)
pause before doing something because you're nervous, embarrassed or worried

image (n)
a picture in your mind

impatient (adj)
annoyed because something isn't happening as quickly as you want or in the way you want

inherit (v)
receive a house or money from someone after they die

injured (adj)
hurt in an accident or attack

in public (phr)
where people in general can see you

in trouble (phr)
in a difficult situation

judge (v)
criticise someone because you think they behave badly

lane (n)
a narrow street

lean (v)
move your body so it is closer to/further from something, usually by bending at the waist; slope in one direction, not be straight/upright

learn your lesson (phr)
be unlikely to do something stupid or wrong again because the last time you did it something bad happened

look onto (phr v)
have a view of

master (n)
a man who has control over servants

meanwhile (adv)
at the same time

mixture (n)
a substance that is the result of mixing different things

mysterious (adj)
not explained or understood

nod (v)
move your head up and down to answer 'yes'

odd (adj)
strange

pale (adj)
with lighter skin than usual because you're ill, shocked or worried

poker (n)
a metal stick used for moving the coal or wood of a fire around

potion (n)
a drink that is magic, poisonous or used as a medicine

relieved (adj)
happy and relaxed because something bad hasn't happened or because a bad situation has ended

reputation (n)
the opinion that people have about how good/bad someone is

safe (n)
a strong metal box with a special lock, used for storing important things

scandal (n)
talk or reports in the newspapers about shocking events involving important people

servant (n)
someone who cooks, cleans or does other work in another person's home

shudder (v)
suddenly shake a lot because you feel frightened

side street (n)
a small street that is connected to a bigger street

sinister (adj)
threatening to do harm or do something evil

sigh (v)
breathe out slowly making a long soft sound, usually because you are disappointed or annoyed

slightly (adv)
a little

split (v)
divide into two or more parts

storey (n)
a level in a building

stroll (n)
a walk for pleasure, without hurrying

suffer (v)
fell pain in your body or mind

suspect (v)
believe that someone has done something bad

suspicious (adj)
believing that someone has done something bad

sweat (v)
produce liquid on your skin when you're hot or nervous

terror (n)
a strong feeling of fear

trample (v)
put your feet down on someone or something in a heavy way that causes injury or damage

transform (v)
become something or someone different

tremble (v)
shake because you're nervous or afraid

trouble (v)
make you feel worried

unscientific (adj)
not done or tested using methods that scientists think are necessary

upright (adj)
straight, not sloping to one side

victim (n)
someone who has been injured or killed as the result of a crime

violent (adj)
using physical force to hurt someone or damage something

whisper (v)
say something very quietly so other people can't hear you

(**whisper**, n)

wild (adj)
(of a person) enjoying parties and having lots of fun; (of weather) with strong winds; (of an animal) not a pet, living in natural conditions

will (n)
a legal document that explains what you want to happen to your money and possessions when you die

www.ingramcontent.com/pod-product-compliance
Lightning Source LLC
Chambersburg PA
CBHW011958090526
44590CB00023B/3780